From:

The Manger and the Message

The Real Story of Christmas in Less Than Two Minutes

Bret Nicholaus

An imprint of William Randall Publishing

William Randall Publishing
P.O. Box 340, Yankton, SD 57078
www.william-randall-publishing.com
Copyright ©2014, 2017 by Bret Nicholaus.
Printed in the South Korea.
All rights reserved. No part of this book may be used or reproduced in any manner whatsoever without the prior written permission of the publisher.
William Randall Publishing's authors are available for seminars and speaking engagements. If interested, please contact us at the address listed above.
Book design by Rick Franklin - rickfranklindesign.com
Images: *pine, © Galina Horoshman, iStock; wood floor, © Bela Tiberiu Attl, iStock; straw, © Claudio Ventrella, iStock; manger, © Adyna, iStock; pine illustration, © Diane Labombarbe, iStock*
ISBN #978-193953212-1

First edition: October 2014; Second edition: October 2017
10 9 8 7 6 5 4 3 2 1

This book is dedicated to my wife, Christina,
and to our two sons, Grant and Luke.

Welcome

What you are about to read is a condensed version of the
Christmas Story—a *really* condensed version! There is,
of course, no proper substitute for carefully and prayerfully
reading the entire Christmas account, especially as it is
recorded in the first couple of chapters of the Gospel of Luke.
It is my hope, however, that this feverishly fast and frank
re-telling of the events surrounding the birth of Jesus—
as well as the truly climactic events that Jesus' birth points to—
will allow you to see with fresh eyes the story of Christ's
coming to this world and his redeeming love for us.

In the midst of this busy, often chaotic Christmas season, may you find *true* peace and joy as you embrace the Good News of Scripture—God's great message of reconciliation and new life.

Note: Corresponding Scripture references have been provided at the end of most stanzas. Please dig deeper into God's narrative as your time allows.

And now, the *real* story of Christmas
in less than two minutes . . .

For Joseph and Mary,
the future's not scary:
They'll be husband and wife,
live a wonderful life . . .

Then an angel appears,
and Mary fears;
she's very confused
by Gabriel's news.

Read it in Scripture: Luke 1:26-29

She's favored by God,
but it all seems so odd.
Did she really hear it?
She'll conceive by the *Spirit*?

Read it in Scripture: Luke 1:30-37

She accepts the fact
and never looks back;
she knows God's hand
is in this plan.

Read it in Scripture: Luke 1:38

Now Joseph's no fool—
somethin' ain't cool!
But an angel of the Lord
gets Joe fully on board.

Read it in Scripture: Matthew 1:18-25

Well, Mary goes out
to Elizabeth's house;
Liz starts to rejoice
when she hears Mary's voice.

Read it in Scripture: Luke 1:39-45

And you may find this funny,
but inside Lizzy's tummy
her own baby boy
begins leaping for joy!

Read it in Scripture: Luke 1:41,44

Then Mary sings praise
and remembers the days
when God spoke to Abe
and foretold of the babe.

Read it in Scripture: Luke 1:46-56

If Rome wants to tax,
you don't rest or relax;
so Mary and Joe
to Bethlehem go.

Read it in Scripture: Luke 2:1-5

This may not be pretty,
but while in the city
their baby arrives
amid cow poop and flies.

Read it in Scripture: Luke 2:6-7

The inn had been full,
and Joe had no pull,
so the newborn is cooing
among braying and mooing.

Read it in Scripture: Luke 2:7

Those with no clout
are the first to find out
that the Savior of all
is in a cow stall.

Read it in Scripture: Luke 2:8-14

The shepherds find the baby,
and at the risk of sounding crazy
they share the angel's story
and give God all the glory!

Read it in Scripture: Luke 2:15-20

The infant is slumbering,
Joseph is wondering,
Mary is thinking,
and the animals are stinking.

Read it in Scripture: Luke 2:18-19

Eight days have passed—
they can name him at last!
Jesus ("God saves") is his name;
to save *us* is the reason he came.

Read it in Scripture: Luke 2:21; 1 Timothy 1:15

'Cause from nearly the beginning,
people had been sinning:
doing their thing
and ignoring their King.

Read it in Scripture: Genesis 6:5; Psalm 14:1-3

They'd cast God aside
and dug a divide;
the chasm was deep,
and the future was bleak.

Read it in Scripture: Isaiah 59:1-2; Ezekiel 7:5-9

With disaster ahead
there was plenty to dread . . .
But his love was too great—
he would no longer wait.

Read it in Scripture: Psalm 130:3-4;
Romans 5:8-10; 1 John 4:9-10

So through divine intervention
God restored the connection,
and the manger—a food trough—
gave way to a crude cross.

---

*Read it in Scripture: 2 Corinthians 5:17-19;
Philippians 2:5-8; 1 Peter 2:24*

You see, the birth of our Savior was only the start
of Jesus Christ drawing us back to God's heart.
Nailed to the cross, he declared his work done;
raised from the dead, our salvation he won!

Read it in Scripture: 1 Peter 3:18;
John 19:30; 1 Corinthians 15:20-23

And this great gift of grace is ours to receive
if with mouths we confess and with hearts we believe
that Jesus is Lord and that God raised him up—
thanks be to God for this wonderful love!

Read it in Scripture: Romans 10:9

So delight in the baby asleep on the hay,
but follow the story the rest of the way:
to the cross, to the grave, to the words "He is risen!"—
the most marvelous message we've ever been given!

---

*Read it in Scripture: Matthew 28:1-9;
Acts 10:34-43*

May the peace and joy of the risen Christ
　　　　　be yours this Christmas and always.

About the Author

Bret Nicholaus is a professional writer
and the author of many books, including
the bestsellers *The Christmas Conversation Piece* and
The Christmas Letters. Bret and his family live
in the Chicago area, where he frequently speaks
at churches, schools, and businesses.